William H. Lyttelton

Church establishments, their advantages, social & religious:

A lecture addressed to the Stourbridge Church of England Young Men's

Association

William H. Lyttelton

Church establishments, their advantages, social & religious:
A lecture addressed to the Stourbridge Church of England Young Men's Association

ISBN/EAN: 9783337727970

Printed in Europe, USA, Canada, Australia, Japan

Cover: Foto ©ninafisch / pixelio.de

More available books at **www.hansebooks.com**

CHURCH ESTABLISHMENTS:
THEIR ADVANTAGES, SOCIAL & RELIGIOUS.

A LECTURE

ADDRESSED TO

THE STOURBRIDGE CHURCH OF ENGLAND
YOUNG MEN'S ASSOCIATION,

BY THE

HON. AND REV. W. H. LYTTELTON,

RECTOR OF HAGLEY AND HONORARY CANON OF

WORCESTER.

PUBLISHED BY THE ASSOCIATION.

LONDON :

BELL AND DALDY.

STOURBRIDGE: T. MELLARD.

1861.

PREFACE.

THE principal political leaders of the dissenters have nonestly declared, before the Committee of the House of Lords, that the abolition of church-rates, for which they are now chiefly agitating, would by no means satisfy them; that it is but a step in the changes which they seek to introduce; and that their main object is the entire separation of Church and State; the withdrawal of all State-support from religion.

Now we have not the slightest fear of their attaining this object for an indefinite number of years, if ever. Nor will any reasonable man complain of their agitating for this purpose, if they sincerely believe it is for the public good. It is, in that case, nothing more than their plain duty to do so; and we rejoice in the fact, that in this country—this almost solitary home of complete political and personal freedom—as we are not afraid to put weapons of war into the hands of all classes of men, so neither are we afraid to allow full liberty to all men to attack any, or every institution of which they disapprove, even though it be one consecrated by the veneration of ages, and forming an integral part of that ancient constitution of this realm, to which more perhaps than to anything else, under God, we owe our truly marvellous national prosperity and greatness. We believe that in an atmosphere of full freedom of discussion, truth will in the end prevail. And an Institution which will not bear the fullest and freest discussion is hardly worth the keeping. But the Church of England will stand far more formidable attacks than any which the Liberation Society, or all her adversaries united can make upon her.

Still, if men attack us, it is right that we should defend ourselves, and be ready to give a reason for our belief and conviction that the union of Church and State, if ordered on sound principles, is in a high degree beneficial to both.

I hope that in this lecture I have not violated Christian charity. I entertain sincere respect for many of our adversaries on this great question. I honour the spirit in which some of their writings—as for instance, Mr. Miall's Eight Letters to the Earl of Shaftesbury—are written. Every one who, like Mr. Miall in these letters—I hope all his writings are in the same spirit—sets an example of courtesy in argument, and of that chivalrous generosity which is so much less common in paper war, than it is in our time in literal war between civilised nations, deserves the thanks of both parties.

But in every time of controversy we shall have instances of war carried on in a very different spirit; there will be demagogues whose object is to ride upon the storm for their own merely personal or party objects ; ministers of the gospel of Divine love, who, professing a theology which declares that " *God is love,*" and that only " *he that dwelleth in love, dwelleth in God,*" set, in common life, deplorable examples of 'that " *odium theologicum* " which has been the scandal of religion in all ages ; who in their churches or chapels make extreme confessions of their own and their party's sinfulness, but out of them confess nothing but other people's ; and who continually urge us to prefer their own system or their own party to that of their antagonists, on the ground of sins in the latter which a moment's serious thought would

shew them were equally, if not more common, on their own side; and in fact belong to human nature everywhere. Mr. Bright's charges against our Church might be retorted with double force upon voluntaryists, as any one may see who will read the evidence drawn from dissenting publications in Dr. S. R. Maitland's admirable little book on the "Voluntary System."

As long as there is sin and error in the world, there must be war; only let all good men labour that the spirit in which the war is carried on be Christian and generous. When men in the violence of party-spirit lose self-possession, they are apt, like the Jerusalem mob, to "throw so much dust into the air," that they can no longer clearly distinguish friend from foe—that which would, in the end, be beneficial to themselves as well as others, from that which would injure them. To attempt to reason with men in this state of mind, is hardly wiser than to appeal to the calm reason of a wild bull charging a red cloak; for it is far more blind animal passion than thoughtful love of God and of man that guides and impels them.

The question here discussed is one in which all good men of every kind are alike interested, since it refers to the best and most effective way of establishing and maintaining the kingdom of our Lord in the world. We do not plead for the *disuse* of the voluntary system; by no means; but only against its *exclusive* use. If we are asked which is the best system for bringing the preaching of Christ's truth and the ordinances of Divine grace within reach of *all* the members of any nation; of the poor as well as the rich; of those who despise, or are indifferent to all religion, as well as of those who value it—for Christianizing a *whole* nation—the Establishment system or the voluntary system—we answer without the least hesitation, that we should use *both* together with all the energy we can.

Those who maintain the sufficiency of the voluntary system by itself, are taking their stand upon unproved theories and gratuitous assumptions, against the universal experience of mankind hitherto.

The following lecture was delivered last year at Stourbridge, and again this year at Bridgnorth. I have endeavoured to make it more worthy of publication—as the Stourbridge Association have wished to publish it—by adding notes, and otherwise, I hope, improving it.

There are some dissenters whom I should never hope to convince. There are men who act upon the principle of one who said, "When I have quite made up my mind, I am ready to listen to argument, because then it can do no harm;" or who, if facts are mentioned which appear to tell against their side of the argument, would answer with a renowned Frenchman, "So much the worse for the facts!"

Upon such men I have no hope of producing any impression. But I cannot conceive how any reasonable man, open to persuasion, can study the subject carefully, without arriving at the conviction that an Established Church, rightly ordered, is one of the greatest blessings any nation can enjoy.

W. H. L.

Hagley Rectory,
April, 1861.

CONTENTS.

LECTURE.

Introduction.

THERE are few subjects of greater importance to us all than that of Church Establishments.

All men who love their church and their country should study it as far as they have means and opportunities; and do their utmost, by conversation and otherwise, to form in the minds of all men an intelligent and well-founded public opinion upon it.

It is no secret that there is in existence a very active society, called the " Society for the Liberation of Religion from State Patronage and Control," whose avowed object it is to sever all connection between Church and State; and which sends out emissaries all over the country to agitate in favour of this great and fundamental change in the ancient constitution of this country.

Now whatever be our opinion upon the desirability or the reverse of such a change, no one will deny that it would be a change of great importance.

Old England without any Established Church would be very different from what it has been with one. If the time should ever come, when tithes being abolished, clergymen will have to go round their parishes asking for subscriptions for the support of themselves and their families; and church-rates being abolished, the willing members of congregations have to pay the whole expenses of the repairs of their church

B

and of the support of its services; and all the other members of the church enjoy its use, free of expense, or paying much less than their fair proportion : the state of things so introduced will be very widely different— whether better or worse is another question—but very different from any we have yet as a nation experienced.

I believe that a thousand characteristics of our quiet English life and our sober English religion, and some of the most valuable features of our peculiar national habits of mind and temper, are the direct effects of the State establishment of a Christian Church, and of nothing else ; though we are very apt to attribute them to other causes, or even to the nature of things. We are so accustomed to many of these advantages, that we are in danger of thinking that they come of themselves. If asked how they arose, many would be ready to make Topsy's answer, " 'Spects they growed." And they think they always would grow, simply because the world is made as it is.

My own conviction on the other hand, and that of many far wiser men, dissenters as well as churchmen, is, that they never would grow, or at least never to anything like their present extent, were it not for the support by the State, as a State, of some Christian Church.

Subject of this Lecture.

Now I intend in this lecture to confine myself strictly to the question of Church Establishments in the abstract. I shall not at all consider whether or no our Church as it is, is the best that could be selected to be established. That is an entirely different question. I only wish to urge that *some* body of Christians ought to be supported by the State.

Stating the case so, you will observe that it becomes no longer a question between churchmen and dissenters. For while on the one hand there are some members of our Church—very ill-judging ones in my opinion—-but still bona fide and earnest members of our Church, who wish to separate Church and State ; on the other hand some of the greatest of the non-conformists of ancient and modern times are strongly in favour of their union. This is an important fact to be urged upon candid dissenters.

Opinions of Great Non-Conformists on Church Establishments.

Matthew Henry, the Independent, one of the best Scripture commentators, writes as follows :—

"Let us give God praise for the national establishment of our religion, with that of our peace and civil liberty; that our Canaan is not a land flowing with milk and honey, but (which is of much greater advantage) that it is Immanuel's land; that the Christian religion—that choice and noble vine, which was so early planted in our land—is still growing and flourishing in it, in despite of all the attempts of the powers of darkness to root it out; that it is refined from the errors and corruptions the Church of Rome had, with the help of ignorance and tyranny, introduced; that the Reformation was in our land *a national act;* and that Christianity, thus purified, *is supported by good and wholesome laws, and is twisted in with the very constitution of our government.*"

Doddridge adds in the same strain—

"Ministers of all denominations claim our prayers, and peculiarly those of established churches; when as the temporal emoluments are generally greatest, there is of course more to invite unworthy persons to offer themselves to the ministry. Nor ought we to forget those wise, learned, and pious men, whom our government may from time to time think fit to raise to the most exalted stations among the clergy, and to invest with a dignity and authority, which, though no part of their ministerial office, is capable of being improved to great advantage. It is devoutly to be wished that they may use their great influence and power to exclude those that are unworthy from that important trust; and that they may preside over the doctrine and behaviour of those committed to their care, in such a manner as may render both most edifying to those who attend their instruction. By these pious and zealous endeavours an establishment will flourish, and separate interests decrease. *But what folly and iniquity were it so much as secretly to wish that one limb might grow by the distemper of the body, or one coast be enriched by the wreck of the public navy.*"[1]

Such was the spirit of these true men of God, among the non-conformists of former days. They were men capable of looking beyond narrow class-interests, and of taking a large view of such questions as affect the whole community.

Let all sober-minded dissenters consider whether Owen, Flavel, Howe, Baxter,[2] Henry, and Doddridge, or the violent party men who compose the Liberation Society, are the likeliest to guide them according to the mind of Christ.

A Church-Rate imposed by Independents.

Here let me notice one remarkable fact with reference to church-rates—that the only Act of Parliament ever passed that imposed church-rates on all parishes (whether, that is, a majority voted for them or not), was in the time of the Commonwealth, when the Church of England was down, and the Presbyterians and Independents held the rule, who then enforced church-rates by Act of Parliament, without either the consent of, or accountability to, the parishioners.[3]

The notion of its being in itself unlawful or unscriptural for the State to support the Church was, I believe, never started by any class of Christians till the end of last century. *All the different professions of faith drawn up in Switzerland or England at the time of the Reformation—twelve I believe in number—urge the duty of the State to support religion.*

Are then our modern Liberation Society sages better authorities on the interpretation of Scripture than all these? Let fair-minded dissenters consider this.

For my own part, I am so earnest a believer in the value of Church Establishments for the due maintenance of religion, and for its diffusion over a whole country, that if our Church were ever to be separated from the State,

(1) Sermon on Deut. xxiii., 9, quoted, together with the passage from M. Henry, in Essays on the Church, p.p. 18, 19.
(2) See their opinions in Note II.
(3) Quoted from Mr. Toulmin Smith, a dissenter, in the Preface to an excellent little tract on the Voluntary System, called "Overbury," by Dr. Molesworth, Vicar of Rochdale, Rivington, p. viii.

I should then earnestly pray that some dissenting body, holding the great essentials of the Christian faith, should be united to it, while we were left to provide for ourselves, as they are now. This however is not a very practical remark. For no one I think whose eyes are not very tight closed indeed to the present state of parties or of public feeling, will imagine that there is the slightest chance that if our Church were separated from the State, any other body of Christians would be united to it in its place. Whatever may be imagined in theory, the only alternative really open to us is, not between the establishment of our own Church and that of some other body of Christians, but between the establishment of our Church or no establishment at all : the present state of things, or the voluntary system.

Let all practical men then make up their minds upon this alternative, and act energetically upon the opinion they arrive at.

Lawfulness of Church Establishments.

I have then now to prove, first, the lawfulness in the abstract, and then the expediency and advantages, social and religious, of Church Establishments.

First, is there anything in itself unlawful or contrary to the will of God as revealed in scripture, or as demonstrated by sound reason, in Church Establishments?

Evidently if there is, there is an end of the question for Christians. What is wrong can never in the end be expedient. We may not bow down to Satan in anything, even if by so doing we could really give all the kingdoms of the world and their glory to Christ.

Argument from the Old Testament.

Now one might have thought that every one would allow that the union of Church and State was allowed, and even commanded, under the Old Testament. For that the Jewish Church was established would appear to be an undeniable fact. But I lately heard this disputed in a lecture delivered by a lawyer, a Mr. Callaway, an eloquent member of the Liberation Society, at Kidderminster.

6

He said that though it was indeed true that it was
the law of God that every one should contribute to
the temple worship, yet no one was *obliged* to obey
that law; that every one who obeyed it did so on the
voluntary system, i.e., by his own will, and not because
he was compelled.

This certainly struck me as an original view. A
law of God, which every one might obey or not as they
pleased, seemed rather a singular thing.

But what was the fact?

The contribution fixed by the law of God to be paid
for the temple and temple worship was half a shekel:
"*This,*" it is said in the law of God, "*they shall give,
every one that passeth among them that are numbered,
half a shekel after the shekel of the sanctuary—every
one shall give an offering unto the Lord. And thou
shalt take the atonement-money of the children of Israel,
and shalt appoint it for the service of the tabernacle of
the congregation, that it may be a memorial unto the
children of Israel before the Lord, to make an atonement
for your souls.*"[1]

"Yes," says Mr. Callaway, "that was the law of God;
but whether a Jew obeyed it or not was, a matter of
choice." Now a matter of choice it was, in the sense in
which all human actions are so; but unfortunately if
he chose the wrong way, he was to be visited with—
what do you think? Nothing short of *the plague!*

Hear the words of the law: "*And the Lord spake
unto Moses saying, when thou takest the sum of the
children of Israel after their number, then shall they
give every man a ransom for his soul unto the Lord,
when thou numberest them, that there be no plague among
them when thou numberest them.*"[2]

Certainly a very peculiar and original "voluntary
system" with this feature in it, that if any one volun-
teered wrong he was visited with the plague! I am
sorry to have to convict Mr. Callaway either of great
ignorance of the subject on which he professed to be a

(1) Exodus xxx., 13-16.　　(2) Ibid. ver. 12.

teacher, or else of as gross unfairness as can well be conceived.

"There are some lawyers in our time, who like their predecessors of old, *"take away the key of knowledge; not entering in themselves, and hindering them that were entering in"* (Luke xi., 52)—use the powers of argument acquired in their professional life to misrepresent the truth; to introduce, instead of exposing, sophistries; to hinder men from seeing plain facts, which would tell against their side of an argument; and so neither ' enter in ' themselves into the world of ' knowledge,' nor allow others to do so. I hope Mr. Callaway does not generally do this, as he has in this case."

It remains then an undeniable fact, that the Jewish Church was in the strictest sense of the term established.

The fabric of the tabernacle first, and of the temple afterwards, was kept in repair; the expense of services in them was defrayed; the Levites who ministered were supported, *by a compulsory rate imposed by the Divine will.*

How much does the Argument from the Old Testament prove?

Such was the case under the Old Testament. How much then does this prove?

Now it is true that the Jewish law and Revelation neither was, nor ever professed to be, perfect or final. Many things, we are expressly taught, were. " winked at'" under it " for the hardness of men's hearts," and because men's natures were not as yet ripe for anything better.

But allowing full force to such considerations, surely no one who is in any sense a believer in the Divine Inspiration and authority of the Old Testament, would refuse to say as much as this : *that none of the great fundamental principles of the Jewish law could have been in themselves immoral.* Not necessarily all that was allowed there is eternally good, nor yet perhaps even every little detail of positive commands; some such things may have had only a local and temporary meaning and force; but no Christian surely will say that any of the great characteristic features of that law to which Christ Himself so continually appeals, could have been in themselves immoral, or contrary to the mind of God.

That wonderful Tabernacle built in the wilderness of this world, the Mosaic Church, must have been made, at least, in its great lines and distinctive features, after a "pattern seen in the Mount;" and all ages and generations cannot have wondered at it ever since, as a marvel of superhuman wisdom—all Christians cannot have believed it to have been of really Divine origin, only for us to listen patiently, while we are told by the great lights of the Anti-State Church Society, that all its great features are "weak and beggarly elements," which such wise men as they have a right to look down upon.

Now whatever else may not have been fundamental in the Mosaic Law, certainly *this* was so : the existence, all over the Holy Land, of an order of men, whose proper work and occupation in life, it was, to keep up the knowledge and worship of God among all the people; and who, for performing this national work, were paid and supported, by Divine command, out of the national funds.

What was this but an Established Church?

The members of the Anti-state Church Society are, of course, bound in consistency to hold that this was a great calamity to the Jewish nation : that the knowledge and worship of God would have been kept up in a much purer and better way, had no such institution, as this National Church, existed; but the Levites had been left, for their support, and the temple and temple services also, to the voluntary subscriptions of the faithful. Individuals might indeed rightly, according to them, "remember the Levite," as the law commanded; but the State, as a State, ought to have forgotten, and taken no notice of them.

The wisdom of Moses, then, and the wisdom of the Anti-state Church Society are here directly at issue.

Which of them is the most truly inspired, I must leave it to you to determine.

For myself, I think, with all my heart and soul,

that it was one of those features in the Mosaic Institutions which most manifestly bore the impress of the Divine wisdom—of the wisdom of Him, who "*needeth not that any should testify of man; for He knoweth what is in man*"—knoweth what this fallen world is, what are its needs, and what the best supplies for those needs; that there should have been provided in it, such an institution·as this duly organized National Church, for the maintenance of the public worship of Almighty God, in the whole country, and in every part of it.

But it may be objected that all that I have hitherto said is drawn from the Old Testament, therefore is not binding upon Christians.

Now I am not sure that there is so much force as many suppose in this objection. For the Old Testament is the only part of the Bible that much professes to deal with such questions. The New Testament is chiefly occupied with other subjects. Great principles of politics are to be derived much more from the law of Moses and the writings of the Prophets, rightly under-　 and interpreted in the spirit and not in the letter,　from other parts of the Bible, which do not so 　ctly bear upon these subjects.

　　Milton, in "Paradise Regained," iv. 357, makes our Lord speak of the Prophets—

> "As men divinely taught, and better teaching
> The solid rules of civil government
> In their majestic unaffected style,
> Than all the oratory of Greece and Rome.
> In them is plainest-taught, and easiest-learnt,
> What makes a nation happy, and keeps it so,
> What ruins kingdoms, and lays cities flat;
> These only, with our law, best form a king."

But still we have not the slightest objection to be tried by the New Testament alone, if our antagonists wish it. We will give them the choice of weapons and of ground; and believe we shall beat them equally on all grounds, and with all weapons, fairly used.

Objections from the New Testament answered.

Now the objections to Church Establishments drawn from the New Testament, are so weak that it is difficult to get firm hold of them.

They most commonly urge against us the many texts in which Christians are exhorted to give *freely*: and then ask whether giving in accordance to a law is giving freely? Where, they say, is the text in the New Testament which speaks of any compulsory payment for ministers or churches?

Now the weakness of this argument is transparent. Because one way of gaining a particular object is commanded, does it follow that all others are unlawful?

Take a similar instance. For one precept urging the voluntary support of the ministry, there are ten urging voluntary contributions for the support of the poor. Of course then, in all consistency, they ought to maintain that all State-interference with this matter also, all legal enactments for the maintenance of the destitute, the aged, or the orphans, are unlawful for Christians, "doing despite," as Dr. Wardlaw has said in the other case, "to all the principles of Christ's Kingdom."

Yet no dissenter, that I am aware of, has ever yet said that poor-rates were unlawful or unchristian.[1]

Surely it is evident that the argument that anything is unlawful simply because we never read of the apostles doing it, is utterly futile. If they had ever *received* an *offer* of this means, and refused it on principle, then indeed the proof would be a good one. But it is well known that the early Christians were never offered any support for the service of God from a Christian government, simply because there was no such government. If they had been offered anything of the kind, I think the whole analogy of Scripture leads us to expect that they would have gladly accepted it.

But then we are asked, "Does not our Lord distinctly say, *My kingdom is not of this world?* Did He not forbid the use of all earthly weapons in defence of His kingdom? Does He not in these words teach, as His apostle afterwards does, that the weapons of our warfare are not to be carnal, but spiritual?"

Doubtless: but does any one understand this to mean that Christ's ministers ought not to receive any money for their support? If so, what shall we say of

[1] "Essays on the Church," p. 36.

dissenting ministers, who are supported by the free gifts of private individuals? Are not dissenting bodies just as truly as our Church, in this sense, an organised "kingdom of this world?" Of course they are. They have a regular system for the provision of funds for the support of their ministers and chapels; and in some cases they have endowments secured by the State.

Dissenters accept of State-aid.

In some cases also they actually accept of State-aid : they have done so in Scotland, in Ireland, and in England, for their cemeteries and mortuary chapels. This is really a very awkward fact for the Anti-State-Church Society. As to rates raised from the whole population for the support of our church, here are dissenters who conscientiously refuse to consent to them; but as to rates equally raised from the whole population—but in this case for the support of their chapels—they equally conscientiously no doubt accept them. Really a most convenient conscience—so delightfully flexible!

Evidently if they agitate to liberate the Church from all her ancient endowments—very many of them, be it observed, endowments from private sources, so they ought to liberate all dissenting chapels from their endowments, and from all State help to their schools or cemeteries.

No individual or nation may *force* religion upon any one; but nations, as well as individuals, are perfectly at liberty, according to all Bible or other principle, to support ministers of religion.

The truth is, it is a marvel that any one should ever have dreamed that our Lord's words to Pilate had anything whatever to do with this subject. What He meant is manifest. He was denying the truth of the common opinion held by the Jews at that time, that, since He had declared Himself to be the Messiah, He must therefore intend to set up an earthly kingdom in opposition to that of Cæsar. If He had so intended, then His servants would have fought to set it up. But what has this to do with the lawfulness or otherwise of Pilate, for instance, or of the Roman Emperor, had he so pleased, giving for the support of ministers of the gospel? The two things have evidently nothing whatever to do with each other.

All the many cases in the Bible History of kings and rulers giving money and help for building temples and supporting churches, are examples of our practice.

Inconsistencies of the Liberation Society.

Let it here be observed that the " London Missionary Society," to which large numbers of dissenters of, I believe, several denominations, *including some members of the Liberation Society,* subscribe, urged upon the king of the South Sea Islands " *the propriety of publicly adopting Christianity as the religion of his dominions ;* " and in another part of their report say that " it is deeply to be lamented that Protestant Governments take little care to convey the knowledge of the true religion, wherever they carry their arms, their commerce, or their arts, in colonization." How very shocking Mr. Miall and his friends must think this ! The fact is, the great bulk of the dissenters do not at all agree with the principles of this Liberation Society.*

Should our Church again begin (as in ages of persecution she no doubt did, though not more than others) to take up arms against the dissenters, or to inflict civil penalties upon them for being dissenters, or in any other way to use physical force to compel them to profess what she considers the true belief; then, indeed, she would rightly come under the charge of contravening these great words of our Lord ; but not so long as her ministers only accept from the nation, as a nation, what all dissenting ministers accept from their own communions, often also from old endowments secured by the State, and sometimes even from the State itself, like ourselves.

Church Corruptions no argument against paying Church-rates, so long as they are the Law of the Land.

Neither is it any solid objection to the payment of church-rates, so long as they are the law of the land,

* See a very remarkable Lecture, delivered at Clifton, against the Liberation Society, by the Rev. J. B. Clifford (Wertheim and Macintosh), price two-pence.

that the Church of England is, according to some, a corrupt Church.

Will any one say that it is more corrupt than the Jewish Church, when our Lord said that the temple was made a "den of thieves;" and when the chief priests and rulers were those who crucified the Son of God? Yet to this Church our Lord paid tribute. On this Matthew Henry, the Independent, observes :—" *Church duties legally imposed are to be paid, notwithstanding church-corruptions. We must take heed of using our liberty as a cloak of covetousness or maliciousness. If Christ pay tribute, do we pretend an exemption?* "[1]

I know of no other argument worth mentioning which has ever been supposed to prove that it is in itself unlawful for a State to support a Church. It seems to me that the argument from Scripture is all on our side : and as to establishing any valid objection to it on the ground of morality, or what is called "the eternal fitness of things," it has not, that I know of, been ever attempted; it would be manifestly impossible to do so.

Expediency of Church Establishments.

I come then now to the next great question, the *expediency* of the union of Church and State. It may be lawful, but is it expedient—good for the church, and good for the nation?

To answer this satisfactorily, you must endeavour to understand clearly the practical differences between the two systems, the voluntary system and the establishment system.

The Territorial and Congregational Systems.

Now Dr. Chalmers, in his admirable lectures on Church Establishments, has shewn that one great difference between the two is, that the latter is what he calls a *territorial*, the former a *congregational* system. Under an Establishment the ministers of some Christian Church have assigned to them, as their proper charge, *all* the inhabitants of a particular geographical district; and every

(1) Matthew Henry's *Commentary*, on Christ paying tribute.

c

part of the country is so assigned by the national government to some minister of Christ. Under the other, or voluntary system, on the other hand, each minister is the minister, not of a district, but of a *congregation*, with which he has become connected by his own voluntarily undertaken efforts, or by the appointment of some body of men, whose authority is not recognised, as in the case of an Establishment, by the whole community, but only by a certain section of it. Observe, therefore, that under this latter system, there may be any number of ministers, in any district, each with his own congregation; but there may at the same time be in that district a number of families, who have not connected themselves with any of these congregations, and to whom therefore none of the ministers have any mission, whose authority is acknowledged by them. This system Dr. Chalmers calls the *congregational* system. To the existence of the *territorial* scheme, some *national* authority—some authority acknowledged by the *whole* nation, is essential.

What then are the advantages to the nation of the territorial scheme?

Consider the clergy first as what Coleridge has called the *clerisy*, *i.e.*, a body of national officers entrusted with the care of the temporal welfare of all members of the nation; and agents for the civilisation of the nation; not *necessarily* even ministers of Christ, though it is far better they should be that also.

Social usefulness of a National "Clerisy."

Now the value is great of this fact alone: that if a clergyman does his proper duty, *he knows all the inhabitants and they know him;* and that he is officially bound to let himself be known to every human being in that district as his friend—not only willing, but in duty bound, to do him all offices of Christian benevolence within his power. What a security this gives that that large proportion of mankind, and specially of English mankind, whose natural reserve and modesty would always prevent their obtruding their personal troubles, difficulties, or sufferings upon others—just the most deserving people— shall be sought out; that they shall have any of their

difficulties, which call for the sympathy and assistance
of neighbours able to give it, made known to those
neighbours; and that in a manner that shall not wound
the feelings of the poor, but shall be felt by them to
be proper and inoffensive.

And with respect not to the receivers, but to the
givers of assistance—what an advantage it is to them,
one for which it would be hard to find any sufficient substitute, that there should be resident in their parish an
educated and intelligent gentleman, whose office obliges
him (at the same time giving him the requisite leisure
and opportunity) to acquaint himself with the real
condition and character of the poor and the suffering,
thereby bringing to their notice all cases of real distress.
If on the other hand the national clergyman happens to
be the only gentleman, the only man of education or
of means, resident in the parish, it is an advantage,
which I think no man of discernment will fail to value
very highly, that at least *he* should be known to all the
poor and the suffering as their friend; that in this
way the upper and more educated classes should be
represented to them in the person of one who, must
almost of necessity be a man at least of professed
benevolence, public spirit, and general kindness. In
many such ways it is hardly possible to exaggerate
the value of a national clergy with territorial charges,
in binding together all classes of society in mutual
acquaintance and good will; in acting as links between class and class; in representing in every place
the national benevolence. Great is the value to the
nation of the parochial system. God grant we may
never find it out by losing it.

Imperfections of the Voluntary or Congregational System.

Now observe how much of all this would be lost
under the voluntary system. Under such a system the
clergyman would not be *obliged* to visit all the inhabitants, and therefore in nine cases out of ten certainly
would not do so. When he had gathered together
what he considered a sufficient congregation, he would
contentedly leave the rest of the population, unless

under some special circumstances, to themselves. If, as in so large a body of men would be certain to be the case with some, one of his chief motives for ministerial effort was the making of a livelihood, the rich would draw more of his attention than the poor. He might indeed be led in order to quiet his conscience to visit a certain number of the poor; but a thousand motives—such as the indolence natural to us all, and which so eagerly lays hold of all excuses within reach to silence the call to work, and which grows upon most men with advancing years;—or the natural modesty and shyness which influences some of the best men most, and which would prevent their venturing upon visits which they could not be sure would be well received; —or again, the notion that a life's work would be more effective, if concentrated upon a small, than if diffused over a large field—these and other motives would prevent all but a very few of the clergy from taking persevering care of *all* the inhabitants of any dis-trict. Besides, it is seldom good for a man to be left to choose his work for himself. Our salvation, I think, generally consists in *not* having our own will in such matters.

Again, that peculiar sense of order and fitness which is so valuable a feature of the English character (how much of it is the direct effect of an Established Church I beg you to consider), would make many families receive the visits of a self-appointed minister much less willingly than that of a nationally-authorised clergyman of the district. Poor and suffering persons, whose self-respect disinclines them to accept of help to which they do not feel they have any proper claim, would rather not encourage visits from such a minister; particularly if they knew that he depended for his living upon the voluntary subscriptions of his congregation, to which they had not the power to contribute. Whereas from the national clergyman such persons have no objection to receive visits, because they know they have a right to his services, and that he is paid by the nation for what he does. Do away with an Established Church, and you will either demoralise the English poor in these high matters, by accustoming them to depend upon charity for spiritual attendance and instruction; or else you will drive them to do without it altogether. The advantage to them of having a ministry provided to which they know they have a right, as members of the nation, is very great. Vicious and ill-disposed persons again, who, under the present system, may often, from fear of a person of recognised official position, be induced to receive the visits of the clergyman, and in the end to profit by them, would without the least scruple shut their doors in the face of any minister on the voluntary system.

Following out this line of thought, I think it will be evident that without such official persons living in our parishes, many would starve who are now sufficiently relieved; many poor men would become secretly embittered against the upper classes, who now learn to look upon them as their sympathising friends and brethren; many rich men and women would lead selfish and idle lives, who now, by the information supplied them by their clergyman, and the claims he makes upon their sympathy and assistance for the poor and suffering, are induced to devote themselves to works of active charity.

I have no such low view of the value of friendship in alleviating the sorrows, and mitigating the sufferings of this suffering and sorrowing world; and no such notion of the commonness of friendship on earth, as to value at less than an almost incalculably high price, the existence of a body of *official friends of all men*, who shall also be ordained ministers of Christ, the great Lover of Souls, the Friend of the poor and the suffering, as well as, and more than, of the rich and powerful.

Usefulness of Country Parsons.

Take away "the parson of the parish" from our out-of-the-way rural districts, you take away the only friend to whom multitudes of the modest poor are in the habit of looking for advice and assistance. Look down from a hill-top (to borrow Cobbett's illustration) upon the remote valleys of rural England, dotted with their solitary cottages—though still in our time, thank God, dotted also with the moss-grown towers of our old parish churches (— how long these will last under the voluntary system, or without church-rates, let our radicals consider), look down, I say, on such valleys, which make up so large a part of the map of Old England; and reflect whether there is the slightest chance of educated gentlemen settling down to the life's-work of educating and spiritualising their inhabitants in more than a very small minority of cases, on any system but that of an Establishment. All the *civilising* agency of a resident clergy (I am not referring here to higher considerations, such as must, however, commend themselves so powerfully to every Christian heart) would soon be withdrawn from the larger number of these, and they would sink into barbarism and heathenism. What the uncared-for residuum of poor, unattached to any self-made congregation, will be in our parishes, on the voluntary system, that will all these out-of-the-way places be in the general map of the country—they will pass unnoticed, or unprovided for.

Consider also the value of this fact—that the Services of our Church are celebrated in all these remote districts—that birth, youth, marriage, death, are accompanied with the noble commentary of our baptismal, confirmation, marriage, and burial services. Every church tower and spire means *this*, among so many other things.

Objections from the faults of the Clergy.

Here however, I can fancy I hear some well-known objections raised, as follows :—"Disinterested friends of all the people indeed ! men of high name and influence, whose presence in any place is a moral and social blessing ! All this is very fine talking; but look at Mr. A., and Mr. B., and Mr. C.,—this parish, and that parish, how will your theory fit them ?"

But let me ask these objectors how is it that according to this uncompromising principle of theirs, they do not abolish the Ministry altogether ? Look at Mr. A., and Mr. B , and Mr. C., among dissenting ministers, multiplied many times over !

It is unworthy of men of sense and honesty to raise such objections. They evidently must, of necessity apply to everything human. All that they come to is simply this—that clergymen are men and not angels. Angels would certainly be very much better; but then unfortunately they are very difficult to get at.

Systems to be judged by their practical results.

But if we are told that we must judge of systems by their fruits, we shall be very glad to accept the challenge ; only let it be, as Dr. Magee has well urged, by their real fruits, as ascertained by experience, not by *a priori* notions of what men think their fruit *ought* to be. Let the characters and lives of any number of clergy of the Church of England fairly selected, be compared with those of the same number of dissenting ministers, and let the result determine which system—that of an Establishment, or that of Voluntaryism, is likeliest to form a body of high-minded, independent, public spirited men, acting fearlessly on Christian principles, and I have not slightest fear what would be the verdict of an impartial jury.

Means used in the Church of England for securing good Clergymen.

Now as to securing good men to fulfil the duties of this, or any office, there are, as far as I can see, only two classes of means which it is possible to use, besides proper education; namely, first, to do all you can to guard against improper, and to secure good, appointments ; and secondly, so to arrange the circumstances connected with the office, as to furnish as many motives as possible to induce the holders of it to fulfil its duties.

Now for the great national work committed to the clergy—the work, I here mean, of attending to the moral, social, and temporal welfare of all members of the nation—we select first, *ministers of Christ*, men, that is, upon whom all the mightiest influences of true religion are brought to bear. And what better means can be suggested for preventing improper persons obtaining ordination, than are already in use in the Church of England? The names of all candidates for ordination are published in Church, in the places where they live, for several successive Sundays. The laity are called upon to come forward and object, if they know anything against them. During the week preceding the ordination, prayers are used in all rightly ordered Churches, that it may please God to guide the Bishops in their appointment of Ministers. The Bishops, Archdeacons, or examining Chaplains are called upon to investigate their character and to examine them. · And as if this was not enough, the Bishop at the time of the ordination, again solemnly calls upon the assembled Church to testify if they know anything against any of the Candidates. Further, when any Minister has been so ordained, before he can receive any appointment he must obtain testimonials to his fitness from three beneficed Clergymen. If any rabid dissenter object that the Bishops and Archdeacons may be worldly, the laity indifferent, the three beneficed Clergymen interested and designing men; the answer is, that such *possibilities* are inevitable in a fallen world. No contrivance of man can prevent some tares growing among all wheat. The true conclusion from these premises is, not that the ministry should be abolished, but that better means should be taken, if any such can be devised, to fill it worthily.

As to the circumstances in which a Clergyman is placed when in charge of a parish, it is difficult to imagine any more fitted to furnish strong motives of all kinds to public spirit, benevolence, and a life of general and impartial beneficence. If you object that even these means often fail; you are only saying, I repeat, that Earth is not Heaven, men not angels.

Incomes of the Clergy.

One more point must be briefly alluded to before leaving this part of the subject. Consider a national clergy, as *holders of national wealth*. If all the money that now goes to the national clergy were to be withheld from them, and otherwise bestowed, would the community at large be a gainer or a loser?

Now on all such questions, you should guard against the gross, though common delusion of supposing that the stopping of such national payments of any kind would enrich the *whole* community. Of course the only gainers are those persons by whom the taxes that produce the money are paid. In the case of tithes, those would be the *landlords.*

If a Bill were passed to-morrow simply stopping the payment of tithes, what would be the effect? Not that *all* classes would be the richer, but only that one very pitiable class, so truly deserving all our compassion—*the landlords.* All the money that used to go to the clergyman of the parish, would then go to the squire. All land would become worth so much more—would fetch so much more in the market; and the ultimate gainers, would of course be the landlords, not the tenants. Which then is the most likely to spend a large per-centage of his money for the general good of the parish, and especially of the poor—a national clergyman or a squire? Supposing they are both on a par in respect of natural good disposition, upon which of the two are the most powerful motives brought to bear, to overcome his natural selfishness or covetousness? Evidently the inducements are far stronger for a clergyman to be liberal to the poor, and to subscribe for public objects, than for a squire to do so. Not to speak of his professed character as a minister of Christ, public opinion expects liberality from him with a force which it requires unusual moral courage to resist. Accordingly it is, I believe, a fact, which the most unquestionable statistics might be brought to prove, that a very far larger per-centage of the income of the clergy is spent upon objects of national benefit—such for instance as the support of national schools, the relief of the destitute, the maintenance of the Houses of God, and the worship of God, than of that of any other class.

This does not shew that they are in themselves better men; it may be only the natural effect of their position. But, if so, this shews the importance of the position. It shews the great value of an order of things which places so large a number of men—holders of a considerable amount of property—in positions which so powerfully incline them to use it in these ways. If the great reservoir of public money is to be poured out, let us pour it upon such recipients as reason and experience would lead us to expect will be the most likely to diffuse its benefits widely.

Now Lord Palmerston, and those who think with him that all men are born good, may perhaps expect that if the tithes were given back to the landlords, they would of their own free will, give as much for public objects;—as for instance, for the maintenance of religion and education in all classes, as the clergy now do. It may be true that this would be the case with some. But anything more contrary to all experience, than such an expectation with respect to most men can scarcely be conceived.

Why not apply the Income of the Church to other public objects?

But if on the other hand you say, "No, do not stop the payment of tithes, but apply them to other national objects"—of course that opens another enormous subject. All I can say on it now is, let us well and wisely make up our minds what these objects are to be, before we proceed to make the change. My own belief is, that the difficulties of the question would in practice be found so great—the claimants for the money so many, that men would give up the business in despair; the end would be, that they would cut the knot, by simply ceasing to collect the tithes—in other words presenting them to the landlords.

But if you ask, why not divide the present income of the national clergy among the ministers of "all denominations?" I answer, for this reason among others, because it would be proved quite impossible to work such a scheme. Where are we to stop? Are we to subsidize the Mormons? or the Secularists? Or if the minister of a congregation of Methodists received pay, and a schism arose among them—a New Connexion was formed—is the minister of this body to receive his share? If not, why not? And then a "Secession from the New Connexion," and soon another from that—the "Old Secession" and the "New Secession?" It needs but a moment's thought to see that such a scheme could not be worked. Those who wish to see the difficulties of it well stated by wise and statesmanlike men, may refer to Dr. Chalmers' lectures, or to Gladstone's Church and State. For my part I had infinitely rather see the Wesleyan Methodists, for instance, made the National Church, and receiving all its funds, while we of our Church received nothing from the State, than any scheme adopted for the distribution of Church property among all sects; simply because I am persuaded that some one National Church, supported by the State, is the only possible provision for *all men*, poor as well as rich, irreligious as well as religious.

However I do not pretend to go fully into that part of the subject; but, to take the lowest ground, I say that at present the holders of this property are most useful national officers, and that till it can be shown that some other application of the money would be as generally useful, it is best to leave things as they are.

It may be well to remind some that the temporalities of the Church are open to be obtained by all classes. A body of national clergy is a distinctly democratic institution; opening a road for men of all classes, even to the highest positions in the State. The late Archbishop of Canterbury was, I believe, the son of a shopkeeper; and the late Archbishop of York the son of a tailor. Many of our bishops are sons of tradesmen. These are facts in which we may well rejoice. Such democracy is a noble feature of our Church.

If the clergy are bad, by all means displace them and appoint others that are better; but do not for that reason destroy the institution. That would be no wiser (to borrow an illustration from Dr. Chalmers) than the act of a man, who, having an admirable system of pipes laid down in his house to bring water into all his rooms, and finding, at some particular time, the water conveyed by these pipes to be bad, should proceed therefore to destroy the pipes! Of course what he ought to do is to keep the pipes, and let good water, instead of bad, be poured through them. Just so, if the clergy who are appointed to convey means of grace, and spiritual, moral, and intellectual instruction and exhortation to every room in this great House of England, are ill-fitted for their high office, do not therefore destroy the institution, but apply it better.

Three Questions to be asked of Political and Ecclesiastical Reformers.

And with respect to all political changes, there are three questions which every wise man will always put to the man who proposes them, namely—

1. What he proposes to set up in the place of what is destroyed?

For if we destroy any existing institution, which, with whatever defects, yet works tolerably well in the world as it is, and set up another in its place which is quite free from those defects, this will be very poor comfort, if it has others which are a good deal worse.

A child, we are told, was so struck with the beauty of the mountains on the horizon that he set off to gather some of the *blue grass.* Unfortunately when he got there, he found the grass much like what he was used to at home; and the country in other respects much less satisfactory to live in. He came back a sadder and a wiser child. Do not be too ready to run after *blue grass;* remember that things are very different in reality and when seen near at hand, from what they may seem at a distance, or as described by men of violent passions and lively imaginations.

2. Whether it is his honest and determined purpose to do his best to set up this other institution in the place of the old? or whether like the fox in the fable, he is only holding out this bait to us to make us leave hold of what we now have, and will be quite content when we have done so, to let us do without the substitute also.

That fox I am credibly informed is not yet dead, or at least he has had many avatars, many incarnations since the days of Æsop, and will, unless I am much mistaken, have many more. A wise man will be on the look out for him under many disguises, especially under that of a popular orator addressing a mixed audience.

3. Whether even if the proposed institution really would be on the whole better than what we now have, and our reformer does honestly intend to set it up in the place of the old, it will be *possible* for him in the present state of things to do so?

For if, while we are living in an old house, which

with many defects, perhaps, and faults, such as unfortunately belong to all human things, yet gives us real shelter from the storms and inclemencies of the world, an enthusiastic person pulls it down, with the benevolent purpose of building us a better one in its place, but unfortunately only succeeds in giving us a magnificent " castle in the air," which cannot, by any contrivance, be brought down to *terra firma*, the result will not be altogether satisfactory! Or if a man proposes, because of the faults in the stone and the timber, to pull down this old house and rebuild it with other stones and timber, which would be a good deal better, only unfortunately such stone and timber is not to be had in the world as it is; but only, say, in the fixed stars, or in an ideal world; or if it does exist on earth, yet we cannot get at it, because between us and it there is a country occupied by unconquerable enemies; then I think we had better not consent to let our old house be pulled down, till some practicable railroad has been laid down to these grand fixed star quarries, and this splendid dream-land.

What we have to ask always is, not only what do men *intend* to give us, but what is there any security that in the present state of things they will be able to give us?

Our old Church has done us good service in her time. Let us not consent to " break down all the carved work thereof with axes and hammers," till we see something better than a pretty picture of something equally good to be set up in her place. If we wilfully cast away great blessings we once had, it is not God's way to give them back easily.

We may *"find no place of repentance though we seek it carefully with tears."* It is not Adam only who, having wilfully cast away a state of privilege he once had, and wishing to recover it, has found a "flaming sword turning every way " keeping the way back.

Religious advantages of the Union of Church and State.

II. I have next to consider the great subject of the directly *religious* advantages of the union of Church and State.

All I have been hitherto saying, would have been almost equally true if these national officers settled in every parish had not been Christian ministers at all, but merely benevolent men, holding an office conferred upon them by the nation, for the promotion of the temporal and social welfare of every member of the nation in that parish. This is one, and a very important view of the subject; but yet every Christian must reckon it infinitely inferior in importance to that view which we have now to consider—that, namely, which looks upon these national officers as ministers of Christ, holding a commission from Christ Himself, and empowered by Him for the fulfilment of their high duties with respect to the spiritual and eternal interests of mankind. Of course I assume that you are men who believe that there are such ministers on earth; that there is a Church of Christ to which the Divine presence is assured. Are there then any advantages which accrue to this Church and to the State respectively from the union of these two, such as they would not enjoy equally were they separated? And if there are such advantages, what exactly are they? These are the questions we have now to consider.

The Church, as a Church of Christ, not dependent upon the State.

Now I do not for one instant believe or allow that the *existence* of our Church as a Church, or even as a powerful and influential Church in this country, depends upon State-support, or upon any such cause whatever. God forbid that we should be guilty of such treason to all our highest faith, of such faint-hearted distrust in Christ's own promises, or in the reality of our Church as a branch of that to which His presence is promised till the end of time. Most heartily do I for my part, and do you, I trust, for yours, subscribe to the noble saying of one whose words have been rightly called "half-battles," I mean that great Christian hero, Martin Luther, when speaking of the grounds of safety of Christ's Church, he said " *Who is the Church's protector, that hath promised to be with*

*her to the end, and the gates of hell shall not prevail
against her? Kings, Diets, Parliaments, Lawyers?
Marry no such cattle."* *

Yes, Martin Luther was not one of those miserable
men, who believe that there is nothing really Divine on
earth; nothing stronger than that the waves and storms
of an ever-changing world could shake or uproot it;
nothing to the existence and permanence of which
the very Word of God is pledged. He was, if ever
there was one, a *religious* man; a man who verily
believed that amid all that changes and perishes in
this visible world, there were some things which
could not perish, because they have their root in God
Himself.

Remember the great words of the 46th Psalm, spoken
of God's ancient Church, and at least equally true of His
Church now, and for ever :—" *God is in the midst of
her, therefore shall she not be removed : God shall help her
and that right early. The heathen make much ado, and
the kingdoms are moved, but God hath shewed His voice
and the earth shall melt away. The Lord of hosts is with
us, the God of Jacob is our refuge.*"

Doubtless, the true strength of our Church is within,
not without—in God, not in man. Therefore nothing
in earth or hell can destroy her. Let her be cast
into the sea, like Jonah she will come up again,
for she is the bearer of a Divine message to mankind;
let her be crucified, dead, and buried, like her Lord,
and let her tomb be guarded by all the force that the
craft and cunning of the world may collect, she will
rise again in renewed glory, and with mightier power.
God will not suffer His Holy One—for in her Divine
character and commission the Church is holy—to see
corruption.

Therefore I, for one, do not for an instant dream
that if the buttresses of State-support were all pulled
down to-morrow, her ancient walls would fall, or for a
moment tremble. No, " *Her foundations are upon the*

* I have given these words as quoted by Coleridge as one of the mottoes to
his treatise " on Church and State." The first part of the quotation alone is a
literal translation of Luther's words—the last words are Coleridge's addition.
But they express admirably the very spirit of many of his sayings.

*holy hills; the Lord loveth the gates of Sion more than all the dwellings of Jacob."**

If all State support were withdrawn from us, we should still remain not only an influential, but far the most influential of all Churches or organised bodies in this land.

Advantages to the Church of Union with the State.

But what then is the advantage to the Church of union with the State? If it is not existence or permanence, what is it?

Extension of Influence.

1. I answer, first, *extension of influence over the whole land and every member of the nation.*

The waters of life contained in the great reservoirs of our Church would still be contained in them, and the reservoirs would remain; but many districts, many human habitations, to which their life-giving waters are now conveyed by the pipes and channels of State-aid, would be deprived of them. This I have already endeavoured to shew.

The Church would lose some influence; and of members of the State and nation, many would lose the benefits the Church now confers upon them, and in a large number of cases would get no substitute whatever for them, but be left in a state of total spiritual destitution.

If any one object that, as it is, our Church does not sufficiently provide for the instruction and edification of all members of the nation; if he draw attention for instance to our great towns, and to the terrible amount of spiritual destitution existing in them; I answer, that this is an argument not for pulling down the Church, but for helping her to extend her influence more than at present she can; to provide, not fewer Churches, ministers, and schools, but *more* of all these. Let our opponents remember that these evils which they are so ready to cast in our teeth, are many of them of their own causing; that, as Dr. Magee has admirably urged, their conduct in this respect is like that of a man

* Psalm lxxxvii. 1.

who should carefully tie our hands and then boast that
we cannot fight. They deliberately and carefully take
off the wheels of our chariots, and then taunt us
because they drive heavily. Such objections are
really not valid against the Establishment system,
but rather against the voluntary system. Why do not
dissenters provide for all these? How is it that their
much-vaunted voluntary system does not reach these
evils? Do we hinder them? Do we forbid the use of
the voluntary system to supplement the deficiencies of
State-aid? Is it not notorious that we profess to be too
glad to make all possible use of *both* systems together,
and that if we are prevented doing as much as
we ought, a large part of the blame lies at the door of
our antagonists, who do all they can to hinder our obtaining the additional help we need for Church-building
and the like?

State-aid then, I say, ought not to be *withdrawn*,
but to be *very much increased*, if we wish the means of
grace to reach all members of the nation. The voluntary system does not do this, and so long as mankind
are selfish and indifferent to the spiritual needs of their
neighbours, never will.

Let it be remembered that with respect to religious
instruction and means of grace, the demand will always
be in inverse proportion to the real need. A large
number of mankind are devoid, not only of all means
of grace, but of all sense of their value. They would
rather pay to get rid of religious ordinances than to
obtain them. "Should we expect thieves to teach
themselves honesty," asks Dr. Hume, "the ignorant to
promote useful learning, or the impure to struggle for
the promotion of chastity? Our missionary operations
abroad are carried on differently. The society at home
provides the means and appliances of public worship for
the Maori of New Zealand, the Zulu of Caffreland, or
the Dyak of Borneo; but for the heathen of our great
towns and cities at home no provision is made.'*

Independence of popularity.

2. But secondly, I come to the great advantage of

* "Condition of Liverpool, Religious and Social," p. 32.

a Church Establishment over the voluntary system; that it makes ministers of religion independent of their congregations.

Nothing can, in many ways, be more mischievous than that a minister's living should depend upon his pleasing his hearers. His duty must often be to find fault with them. That must be a vicious system, which makes those, the very purpose of whose life is to be to try to raise men above their natural state, dependent upon pleasing them *in* their natural state. Instead of Felix trembling before Paul, you have in such a case, it has been truly said, Paul trembling before Felix.

Some dissenters are, I must say, shamelessly unfair and dishonest in their arguments upon this point. They urge that the clergy of the Established Church are not free or independent-minded, because they are dependent upon the State; and therefore they urge that they should be reduced to the condition, in this respect, of dissenting ministers. Are then their own ministers altogether independent-minded? Which, let me ask, is the worst or most oppressive control, that of the State, such as it is, over us of the national clergy (and, in all sincerity, I do not know what it is; I have no notion of feeling in the slightest degree dependent upon the State, with respect to my doctrine or ministerial practices)—but, I ask, which is the most oppressive control, that of the State over us of the national clergy, or that of their own congregations, or their own deacons, over the ministers of dissenting chapels? Surely the tyranny of a mob may be a thousand times more oppressive than any other. On the voluntary system all clergymen would be dependent, if not literally upon the will of a mob, yet upon the votes of a majority. The object of the Church of God is to reform the world after the model of Christian doctrines and precepts; but the effect of the voluntary system would be to reform Christian doctrines and precepts by universal suffrage. What kind of religion would the world vote for? Is it likely to be very elevating? Are the most popular preachers just the men to do the most substantial good? Would you wish for a state of things, in which you would have

Christ's ministers, as it has been said, "crying up each their wares, and bidding against one another for popular favour?"

Of course I know that very many men would still, under any system, be found strong enough, and noble-minded enough by the grace of God, to stand firm against such temptations. I am glad to bear witness to the noble and truly Christian lives of many a dissenting minister, in the face of all such temptations. But I am speaking of the effect certain to be produced upon average men, such as will always constitute a large proportion of any class of mankind. I say that the effect of the voluntary system upon the doctrinal and practical teaching of such men would inevitably be very lowering. And if you feel and acknowledge the vast practical importance of conferring upon our judges such an income as will raise them above the allurements of bribes, then be sure it is at least equally important for the sound education of any country to raise its moral and religious teachers above the danger of corruption in any form; especially above that most powerful temptation to which a teacher is exposed, who knows that his very livelihood, and that of his family, may be taken from him if he displeases his hearers. God forbid that the time should ever come when the moral and re-ligious teachers of our country shall be subjected to such a trial of their courage and constancy.

And I believe one great reason why clergymen are oftenest, I honestly think, less bigoted, more fair-minded, more tolerant, than dissenting ministers, is, that they have not to fight for their position. Their position is a settled and acknowledged one. They need not to be continually asserting their rights; and so have more time to act upon them quietly. Whereas many men, and especially leaders of sects, are so occupied with disputing in favour of their own peculiar views in religion, that they have comparatively little time left to give to those great fundamental truths in which almost all Christians agree. And just as one great advantage of the possession of wealth is, that it delivers a man from the necessity of continually thinking about money; and a great advantage of having an established rank and

position in society is, that it delivers a man from the
degrading and vulgarising temptation to be continually
pushing for precedence; so is it an invaluable advantage for religion that we have a set of men in the
country whose religious position is acknowledged and
established, and who are therefore at leisure, quietly
and uncontroversially, to meditate upon the great doctrines of religion, to live upon them, and teach others
to do the same.

Appeal to all Christians in favour of Church Establishments.

Finally, we appeal also on higher grounds to all
Christians, to support a national profession of Christian belief. I say to *all* Christians; for it is, as I have
said, almost only *modern* non-conformists who have
denounced, or not strongly advocated, *some* National
Establishment of religion. Some of the greatest names
in the annals of non-conformity—and how could I mention greater than Owen, Howe, Flavel, Doddridge,
Matthew Henry—are on our side in this argument.
They would have preferred, no doubt, to have seen
the body to which they themselves belonged united to
the State; but failing this, they were not only content,
but eager to see our Church united to it rather than
none. I appeal then to fair-minded Dissenters to
listen thoughtfully to our arguments; and if the result
should be to bring them over to the opinions of these
their great forefathers in the faith, then if they have
largeness of mind and generosity of spirit to be able to
rise, as they did, above mere party or sectarian feeling,
let them have the courage to stand firm against their
own party-leaders.

Lay no rash hands upon that old and venerable tree,
which has struck such deep roots in the whole soil of
our country; which, through so many centuries, has
grown with her growth and strengthened with her
strength; under whose mighty shelter so many of the
noblest of her sons have been nurtured; lay no hands I
say upon this tree of God's planting, unless you see your
way not only to plant, but to make to grow in its place

in this our modern world another tree which shall furnish as effective a shelter for whatever is highest and noblest on earth.

Is it nothing to a Christian to see that under the present system all great acts of State are accompanied with solemn religious services; that the Coronation of our Sovereigns is celebrated in one of our great National Churches; that Royal Proclamations and great acts of the State are prefaced with words of high Christian faith; that the debates in Parliament are still opened with prayer; that the Sovereign Ruler of the Land is still, in one true sense, always "most religious," however unworthy some of our Sovereigns (though not, thank God, our present noble Queen) may be of the title; because it is only after a solemn profession of religious faith, and a vow that he, or she, will support the Protestant Faith, that they are admitted to the supreme office; that, in short, the State, as a State, is still professedly and openly Christian? Yet how could all this be under the voluntary system? Will you commit the celebration of State services to all sects in turn? Would this be tolerable to any of us? No, the only alternative to the present system is that, under which the State *professes entire indifference to all forms of religious belief, and therefore dispenses with all religious services of every kind.*

I ask whether that will not be a miserable day, if it ever comes, which God forefend, when all these sacred ceremonies and sacraments of faith, to which I have alluded, are swept away; and one only subject is forbidden, and shut out from State acts, and State ceremonies, namely, that one subject, which alone gives glory and true greatness to all the rest—the subject of religion, and the worship of our God and Saviour.

Depend upon it, if you value justice and truth in high places; if you value a high tone in public men and public functionaries; if you wish to make sure that men as men shall be respected, that the true equality of mankind before God shall be maintained; if, further, you wish that the great truths of religion shall be taught to all members of that lowest stratum of society in which earthquakes originate, and that these shall all of them be taught that reverence before the Eternal Power that governs all things, which alone saves us from the terrible evils and desolations of rebellion and revolutions— by teaching men that it is not in the power of man to new-make the world according to his own fancies, or to get rid of evil and suffering by violence and self-will— then the best way to gain all these great objects is to maintain the solemn profession of the faith in the whole land; and to make its maintenance everywhere to depend not upon the fluctuating fancies of the people, but upon the fundamental laws and constitution of the realm.

One security only is there for the prosperity and nobleness of nations, that is, true religion. The arm that is stretched out without this, however strong it may seem, shall in the end wither; every arm that is stretched out *with* it shall, however weak it may seem, prove in the end mighty for good. Let Moses hold up his arms in prayer on the mountain-top, and Amalek shall be defeated; let him suffer them to fall, and Amalek shall prevail. This is our firm belief. Of this we believe the whole course of human history and experience, as well as the Bible itself, demonstrates the truth. And for the keeping alive of religion in a whole country, I maintain that infinitely the best means is the union with the State of some one Christian Church.

And if in our noble Liturgy we pray that " peace and happiness, truth and justice, religion and piety, may be established among us for all generations," one principal sense in which all wise lovers of their country should use these words is, that it may please God to preserve ever among us a national profession of religion, a national Christian Church; for that is the truest foundation of peace and happiness, truth and justice, religion and piety, in the *whole* nation. Reform and enlarge that which you have, if you will and if you can; but beware of forsaking her, lest God's blessing in more ways than you dream, forsake you.

I cannot conclude better than in the noble words of one of the greatest men whom God has of late years given to this country and to the world, whom no one will suspect of being actuated by anything but an impartial love of truth, and a high-minded patriotism, I mean the poet Wordsworth. Hear how that great man spoke of the Church as well as the State, of England, and of their union :—

> Hail to the Crown by Freedom shaped to gird
> An English Sovereign's brow—and to the Throne
> Whereon he sits ! whose deep foundations lie
> In veneration, and the people's love ;
> Whose steps are Equity, whose seat is Law.
> —Hail to the State of England ! and conjoin
> With this a salutation as devout,
> Made to the spiritual fabric of her Church ;
> Founded in truth ; by blood of martyrdom
> Cemented ; by the hands of Wisdom reared
> In beauty of holiness, with ordered pomp,
> Decent and unreproved. The voice that greets
> The majesty of both, shall pray for both ;
> That mutually protected and sustained,
> They may endure as long as Sea surrounds
> This favoured land, or sunshine warms her soil.

END OF LECTURE.

NOTES.

Note A.—*On Party-Spirit.*

The following striking passages from Archbishop Whately's Bampton Lectures, on Party-spirit, may be useful at a time of controversy such as the present:—

"The great historian of Greece (Thucydides), who described with such frightful vividness of colouring the political party-spirit of his own times, and who pronounced, with the prophetic power which results from wide experience, acute observation and sound judgment, that the like would be ever liable to recur, though in various forms and degrees, has proved but too true a prophet. Much of his description may be applied with very slight, or without any, alteration, to many subsequent periods, not excepting the present.........No assurance," he says, "or pledges of either party could gain credit with the other; the most reasonable proposals, coming from an opponent, were received, not with candour, but with suspicion; no artifice was reckoned dishonourable by which a point could be carried; all recommendation of moderate measures was reckoned a mark, either of cowardice or of insincerity; he only was accounted a thoroughly safe man whose violence was blind and boundless; and those who endeavoured to steer a middle course were spared by neither side."—*Whately's "Bampton Lectures,"* p. 57.

In another place the Archbishop says:—

"Of the baneful *effects* of party-spirit, the most obvious and the most shocking, is the extinction of Christian charity—of that spirit of meekness, forbearance, and benevolence, which are characteristic of the gospel. If one should go through Paul's description of charity, reversing every point in the detail, he would have no incorrect description of party-spirit, as it has appeared in almost all ages of the Church. Party-spirit is *not* 'long-suffering nor kind;' party-spirit 'envieth, vaunteth itself, is puffed up,' making men feel a pride in their own party and hostile jealousy towards all others. 'Party-spirit seeketh her own' (narrowing men's views to the welfare of their party, and inclining them to sacrifice the interests of all others to it); 'party-spirit is easily provoked: thinketh evil' (being ever ready to attribute to an adversary the

E

worst motives and designs); 'rejoiceth in iniquity, and rejoiceth
not in the truth;' catching eagerly at every unfair advantage, and
leading to an indifference about gospel-truth, which was the object
originally professed."—*Ibid.* p. 65.

NOTE B.—*Books and Pamphlets upon the present Controversy.*

Abundant facts proving the insufficiency of the voluntary
system in providing means of grace for the United States of
America, will be found stated with admirable ability and clearness
by Dr. Magee, in his pamphlet on the "Voluntary System;"
which it is not too much to call one of the most masterly and
satisfactory ever published on any subject. The same question is
also ably treated in "Essays on the Church." The statistics
given by these two writers, proving the deplorable failure of
the voluntary system, may, I suppose, be trusted, since they
are all gathered from the writings of strong advocates of that
system. Its working among dissenters is also exhibited in
a vast number of facts compiled by Dr. S. R. Maitland (who
was himself brought up a dissenter) entirely out of dissenting publications, in his excellent, clever, and entertaining book,
called "The Voluntary System"—a good book for lending
libraries.

A striking picture of some of the evils of voluntaryism—of the
tyranny of the "deacons" over their ministers is given in a little
sixpenny publication of Dr. Molesworth, of Rochdale, called
"Overbury," published by Rivington.

The Free Kirk of Scotland, which is sometimes mentioned as
an instance of the success of the voluntary system, is nothing of
the kind. It is a richly endowed church; and its members are
strong advocates for the union of Church and State, wherever it
may be purchased without the sacrifice of any great principle.

I need hardly mention that thoughts of the highest value on
this whole subject may be found in Gladstone, *On Church and
State,* as well as in Dr. Chalmers' lectures. The publications of
the Manchester Church Defence Association, (Sowler and Son's,
Manchester,) are also useful. On the other side of the question,
Dr. Wardlaw's lectures and the publications of the Liberation Society are, I believe, the principal authorities.

NOTE C.—*Opinions of Non-Conformists in former ages in
favour of Church Establishments.*

The notion that the State ought not to meddle with religion,
and that Church Establishments are injurious to religion, is of
modern origin.

Dr. Owen, one of the very greatest of the Puritan Divines,
preaching before the Long Parliament, says:

"If it comes to this, that you shall say you have nothing to
do with religion as rulers of the nation, God will quickly manifest
that He hath nothing to do with you as rulers of the nation.
Certainly it is incumbent on you to take care that the faith which
was once delivered to the Saints, in all the necessary concern-

ments of it, may be *protected, preserved, propagated,* to and among the people over which God hath set you."

John Howe, another great name, in his sermons on the yet future, but expected prosperity of the Church, looks to see this prosperity brought about, "First, by means of the kings and potentates of the earth—and think how it will be if such Scriptures come to have a fuller accomplishment than they have ever yet had; when in all parts of the Christian world kings shall be nursing-fathers, and queens nursing-mothers; when the Church shall suck the breasts of kings; when the glory of the Gentiles shall be by them brought into it. Think whether this will not do much to the making of a happy state, as to the interest of religion in the world," etc.

Flavel, in his exposition of the Assembly's Catechism, replies to the question, "What is the duty of political fathers or magistrates, to their political children or subjects?" in the following words: "It is to rule and govern the people over whom God hath set them, with wisdom; *carefully providing for their souls in every place of their dominion." "And they taught in Judah, and had the book of the law of the Lord with them, and went about through all the cities of Judah, and taught the people."* (2 Chron. xvii., 9.)

Richard Baxter, in his Christian Directory, when addressing civil rulers, says: "Let none persuade you you are such terrestrial animals, that you have nothing to do with the heavenly concernments of your subjects. There is no such thing as a temporal happiness to any people but what tendeth to the happiness of their souls; it must be thereby measured, and thence estimated....... The very work and end of your office is, that under your government the people may live quietly and peaceably, in all godliness and honesty."

"So entirely opposed, then, were all these truly great men, in whose well-earned reputation the dissenters of modern days delight to clothe themselves, to that notion which has of late been promulgated, of the anti-christian nature of the alliance between Church and State."

I have extracted these passages from an able and useful book—though disfigured, as I think, by bitter attacks upon opinions held by some of the most eminent men and most earnest Christians in our Church—"Essays on the Church, by a Layman," published by Seeley.

Note D.—*Christianity never filled whole countries till supported by the State. Dr. Chalmers' final verdict on Voluntaryism.*

Dr. Chalmers has well stated this part of the argument in the following striking passage, quoted in Essays on the Church:—"It is a far mightier achievement than may appear at first view, completely to overtake the length and breadth of a land. All the devices and traverse movements of the many thousand missionaries who, during the first three centuries, lived and died in the cause, failed in their accomplishment. I beg you to recollect that fact, because it is one of chief importance in the argument for a religious establishment—that, notwithstanding the high endowments, the political endowments—notwithstanding the advantages of highly-gifted men, though bordering on the ages of inspiration—yet all the movements in the three first centuries did little more than plant Christianity in the *cities* of the Roman empire. And that is the reason why the term "heathen" is synonymous with that of "pagan," which signifies "countryman;" it was because the great bulk of the countrymen (and those who lived in the country) were still in this state of heathenism. These men did much in the work of spreading the gospel externally, but they left much undone in the work of spreading it internally. They had Christianized the thousands who lived in cities; but the millions of pagans, or the peasantry, who were yet unconverted, evince the country to have been everywhere a great moral fastness, which, till opened up by an establishment, would remain impregnable.

"Now this very opening was presented to the ministers of Christ when the Roman Emperor, whether by a movement of faith, or of philanthropy, or patriotism, made territorial distribution of them over his kingdoms and provinces, and assigned a territorial revenue for the labourers of this extensive vineyard; and so enabled each to set himself down in his little vicinity, the families of which he could assemble to the exercise of Christian piety on the Sabbath, and among whom he could expatiate through the week in all the offices of attention and Christian kindness.

"Such an offer, whether Christianly or politically made on the one side, could most Christianly be accepted and rejoiced in by the other. It extended inconceivably the powers and the opportunities of usefulness; it brought the gospel of Jesus Christ into contact with myriads more of imperishable spirits : and with as holy a fervour as ever gladdened the breast of the devoted missionary, when the means of an ampler service in the Redeemer's cause, were put into his hands, might the Church in these days have raised to heaven her orisons of purest gratitude, that kings had at length become its nursing-fathers, and opened up to us the plentiful harvest of all their populations."

If it be objected that Dr. Chalmers himself by joining the Free Church gave up the support of the Establishment-principle, and gave in his allegiance to the voluntary principle, I answer this is a total misrepresentation of the case.

The advantages, as he considered them, of the union of Church and State, great as they were, were not indeed to be purchased at all costs—not, for instance, at that of the surrender of any great principle. It might be *necessary* to separate the two ; but if so, the necessity would be a deplorable one. That this was Chalmers' final verdict upon the question will be seen from the following words, written at the end of his life :—

"I can afford to say no more than that my hopes of an extended Christianity from the efforts of voluntaryism alone, have *not* been brightened by my experience since the disruption.

This is no reason why we should seek an alliance with the State by a compromise of the Church's spiritual independence; and still less with a government which, on the question of endowments, disclaims all cognizance of the merits of that religion on which it confers support, and makes no distinction between the true and the false, between the scriptural and the unscriptural. Still, it may be a heavy misfortune—it may prove a great moral calamity —when a government does fall into what, speaking in the terms of my own opinion, I hold to be the dereliction of a great and incumbent duty. And ere I am satisfied that voluntaryism will repair the mischief, I must first see the evidences of its success in making head against the fearfully increased heathenism, and increasing still, that accumulates at so fast a rate throughout the great bulk and body of the common people. We had better not say too much on the pretensions or the powers of voluntaryism, till we have made some progress in reclaiming the wastes of irreligion and profligacy which so overspread our land ; or till we see whether the congregational selfishness which so predominates everywhere can be prevailed on to make larger sacrifices for the Christian good of our general population........The Free Church is at this moment lifting a far more influential testimony on the side of ecclesiastical endowments than can possibly be given in any other quarter of society."—*Memoirs of Dr. Chalmers*, Vol. iv., 488-90.

Note E.—*On the Incomes of the Clergy.*

A favourite topic with all enemies of the Established Church is its wealth. Popular orators are continually drawing attention to the riches of Bishops and dignataries; to the millions a year belonging to the clergy as a body ; to the thousands out of these millions that go to the Bishops; and the miserable pittances allotted to some working curates.

Now of course all such facts are admirable for drawing cheers from a public meeting, mainly composed of those who are not accustomed to take the trouble to look deeper than the surface of things, or carefully to analyse large statements, or the particulars of which they are made up.

But what are the facts?

Mr. Callaway, in his lecture at Kidderminster, estimated the whole income of the clergy at five millions a year. The number of the clergy is I believe 17,320. The five millions divided equally among these will give an average of £289. Will any one say this is too much to give such men as the national clergy ought to be? It is, I am told on good authority, less than the average income of ministers of the Church of Scotland.

I do not by any means deny that some reform is needed in the Church as to the distribution of Church-revenues. The incomes of the Bishops have lately been very much reduced; greatly to the benefit of the Church. And a better division of the incomes of the rest of the clergy might, doubtless, be made, and some great abuses remedied.

But what would be the effect of dividing the money equally? In the first place, would the public benefit by it? Is it not evident that a clergyman with £289 a year would be *obliged*, if he was married and had a family, and would be very much tempted even if he were a single man, to spend the whole of that very moderate income upon personal and private objects? Whereas the effect of giving larger incomes to Bishops and dignitaries is, that a large per-centage of them is given away for public objects. Let the subscriptions given in any year by Bishops and dignitaries to public objects, to church-building, schools, and almsgiving, be counted, they will be found an enormous sum. I know of one Bishop who gave in a single year a quarter of his whole income to churches, schools, and parsonages, besides what had gone for other charitable objects. Now most of this would have been lost to the public on the levelling system. Look down subscription-lists for charitable purposes, you will find in most cases that a large proportion comes from the clergy. The census on education (on which, as Dr. Hume—to whom I am indebted for many of my facts—has said, political dissenters maintain a most eloquent silence) shews that the Established Church *educates four-fifths of the children of the poor.*

As to the expediency of conferring wealth and high station on Bishops, hear Edmund Burke:—"Whilst we provide first for the poor, and with a parental solicitude, we have not relegated religion (like something we were ashamed to shew) to obscure municipalities or rustic villages. No! we will have her to exalt her mitred front in courts and parliaments. We will have her mixed throughout the whole mass of life, and blended with all the classes of society. The people of England will shew to all the haughty potentates of the world, and to their talking sophisters, that a free, a generous, an informed nation honours the high magistrates of its Church; that it will not suffer the insolence of wealth and titles, or any other species of proud pretension, to look down with scorn upon what they look up to with reverence; nor presume to trample on that acquired personal nobility which they intend always to be, and which often is, the fruit, not the reward (for what can be the reward?) of learning, piety, and virtue. They can see, without pain or grudging, an Archbishop precede a Duke. They can see a Bishop of Durham, or a Bishop of Winchester, in possession of ten thousand pounds a year; and cannot conceive why it is in worse hands than estates to the like amount in the hands of this earl or that squire; although it may be true that so many dogs and horses are not kept by the former, and fed with the victuals which ought to nourish the children of the people." "We shall believe those reformers then to be honest enthusiasts, not, as now we think them, cheats and deceivers, when we see them throwing their own goods into common, and submitting their own persons to the austere discipline of the early Church."—(From *Burke's Reflections on the French Revolution.*)

Which are we to account the wisest politicians, Edmund Burke, Gladstone, Chalmers, or the leaders of the Liberation Society?

Depend upon it, if we have pedestals of public honour and of commanding influence in the country, we shall not, if we are wise, overthrow any of them; we shall only labour to get the right men set upon them. If we can do that, the larger the number of such pedestals we have, the better for us all.

That our present system of patronage is not the best possible, —far indeed from it; that we may even sometimes wish for a Church-Garibaldi to deliver us from it, I should be one of the last to deny. But this is not a reason for abolishing the union of Church and State, but for ordering it better;—for giving the Church greater power to speak her mind in Convocation, or otherwise. But though our system of patronage is bad, it is incomparably better than that which prevails in many chapels under the voluntary system. Dr. Maitland and Dr. Magee have brought to our knowledge most grievous facts on this subject. Nothing is easier than to find fault with systems of patronage while in "opposition;" nothing more difficult than to find a good one, free from the enormous evils of canvassing, while on the "other side of the House."

In a very remarkable pamphlet by the late Mr. Cawood, of Bewdley, called "*The Church of England and Dissenters*," (Seeley's) price 1s. (well deserving of distribution by Church Defence Societies), a terrible exposure will be found of the evils of the voluntary system, as it exists among dissenting communities, in extracts drawn from a book entitled "*Christian Fellowship, or the Church Member's Guide*," by the eminent Independent, the late Mr. Angell James. · The extracts are from the second edition of the book—some of the later editions having, I understand, been judiciously *expurgated*, on account of what was considered the dangerous candour of its disclosures as to the real state of many dissenting communities. In this book Mr. Angell James states that, in the election of ministers in dissenting chapels, sometimes "*only trustees vote;*" (it is of course all done by *vote*, on the voluntary system) some, times "*only male subscribers;*" sometimes "*female subscribers;*" and sometimes "seat-holders generally, *including Arians and Socinians!*" He says that the choice of a new minister "*always* brings on a *crisis* in the history of the (vacant) church." At this "perilous crisis," "secret canvassing," "cabals, intrigues, and the *most disgusting exercise* of the most *disgusting tyranny*" between opposing "parties take place." Some "deacons make kindness and assistance a cloak for their own tyranny; or a silken web to wind round the *fetters* they are preparing for the *slavery of their pastor!*" For "what is the deacon of some of our dissenting communities? the *patron of the living*, the *Bible of the minister* (*i.e.* as guiding his doctrines), and the *wolf of the flock.*"

Much to the same effect might be quoted; and after stating some of the worst abuses he adds "lamentable state of things! *would God it rarely occurred!*" Let it be remembered that these are not my words, but those of a dissenting minister of the most unquestionable trustworthiness and high character. Is this the system of Church patronage that we are exhorted to substitute for our own?

There are many and great evils in the government of our Church, and in its systems of patronage ; but there are none at all comparable to these.

NOTE F.—*On compulsion to pay Rates under the Old Testament.*

In answer to my statement that the payment of rates for the maintenance of religious worship among the Jews was compulsory, inasmuch as it was enforced by a penalty of the plague on disobedience, Mr. Callaway in a letter to the *Bridgnorth Journal* replies : " that Mr. Lyttelton's argument was based upon a misapprehension of what ' compulsory ' and ' voluntary ' meant. That the compulsion voluntaries objected to was, of course, *human* compulsion. That when God commanded the payments *He* threatened to punish disobedience, and gave no permission *to man* to enforce His claim. That is the true voluntaryism, and no " peculiar kind," which holds that every man is to obey what he thinks is God's law, and is responsible alone to the Almighty ; and that no man or government has a right now to usurp God's place, and use a compulsory power which God did not even give to Moses. This is why I called the Jewish payments voluntary."

So that Mr. Callaway believes that though it was indeed the law of God—disobedience to which was to be visited with a national visitation of the plague—that every man should pay this rate, yet if any Israelite deliberately refused to obey that law, the Jewish authorities would have allowed him to do so with impunity so far as man was concerned, and would have left him to God's judgment.

This is so paradoxical an opinion as hardly to need an answer. The infliction of punishment was certainly not ordinarily left to the Almighty.—See Deut. xvii., 8-13 ; Lev. xxiv., 13-16, and many similar passages. In the former passage the reason assigned for *putting a man to death,* is that he "*did presumptuously, and would not hearken unto the priest that stood to minister before the Lord God, or unto the judge,*" nor act "*according to the sentence of the law which they taught.*" Such a man was not to be left to God's judgment miraculously inflicted, but was to be *executed by the civil power.*

The truth is, that though the Jewish laws were far more merciful than those prevalent in heathen countries, they had nevertheless a character of terrible sternness.

As to punishments inflicted by the civil magistrates, among us, or in any country, for wilful disobedience to the law of the land, it is evidently a great misuse of words to call such punishments " persecutions," merely because some think the law a bad one. *So long as it is the law,* it must be enforced. The magistrate is bound to enforce it ;—whether by " seizing the man's clock," or in some other way, must depend upon circumstances. To allow any one to disobey a law because he thinks it an unjust one, is simply to give up government altogether, and to let every man do "*that which is right in his own eyes.*"

One might have thought a lawyer would have understood

such a first principle of politics ; and would not have branded as "persecution" acts done by magistrates and official persons—whether the acts consist of "seizing clocks," or of any similar strong measures—in compelling " *tribute to be paid to whom tribute is due."* Whether the receiver of the tribute be a Nero, as in the days of St. Paul, or a King Alfred, and whether he spends it well or ill, has nothing whatever to do with the question. It may be a reason for changing the government ; it is no reason at all for refusing to pay tribute to it while it is the government —unless indeed in a case so bad as to make rebellion justifiable. Neither is any man in the slightest degree responsible for the use to which Government applies any tax. The Government alone is responsible for that.

These are some of the most elementary of all truths of political morality.

NOTE. G.—*On the " Territorial" System. A specimen of Claptrap made to do duty as Argument.*

The following comment made by Mr. Callaway upon the part of my lecture referring to the "territorial system " is a good specimen of the kind of argument popular orators think good enough for public meetings :—"To carry out the Hon. and Rev. gentleman's proposition, namely, the 'territorial system,' " said Mr. Callaway, at Bridgnorth, "the Church should commence a crusade against the dissenters. They should banish the Presbyterians, hang the Independents, drown the Baptists, give no quarter to the Primitive Methodists, smite the Quakers—clear all sects, root and branch out of the land (applause and laughter); then the territorial principle could be carried out, but not otherwise."

When in controversy one of the combatants ceases to use argument, and begins instead to throw any mud that may be within his reach at a man of straw, whom he wishes his audience to mistake for his antagonist, we may make excuse for him, but it is only on the score of loss of temper, or of great frivolity of mind. Such missiles recoil in the end with double force upon the man who lowers himself and his cause by making use of them.

Did Mr. Callaway really think that a system which should tolerate only one class of Christians, and exterminate all others by physical force, was the same as one which merely assigns pecuniary support to one, and withholds it from others? Not in the least; he could not have thought so for a moment. But he thought this style of argument good enough for a popular audience.

It is not a satisfactory excuse for " *casting about fire-brands, arrows, and death,"* or even irrelevant jokes on grave subjects, to say " *am not I in sport?"* (Prov. xxvi., 18, 19.) The folly and sin is to "be in sport," or to encourage others to be so, on such matters.

It is to be hoped that the progress of sound education will introduce more and more men into every public meeting who are

not to be caught by such clap-trap (a " *trap*" with which to catch
the " *claps* " and cheers of the foolish or thoughtless) and will receive it, not with " applause and laughter," but with the indigna-
tion it deserves. On the particular case in question, let it be
remembered that the great advocate of the " territorial system "
in church-matters was—and unless Mr. Callaway was entirely
unacquainted with the literature of his subject he must have
known it—that cruel and narrow-minded persecutor Dr. Chalmers!
Let all honest men combine to put down this style of controversy on grave matters, whether used on their own side of the
dispute, or on that of their antagonists. Under a representative
government the habit of mind it fosters may have serious con-
sequences.

Note H.—*The Church's right to her Property. Opinions of
.Dissenters on Endowments for religious purposes.*

I have spoken of the property of the Church as if it were a *gift*
from the State, a kind of salary continually voted by the nation
to the officers of the National Church. But evidently this is not
a complete statement of the case. A large part of the property of
the Church comes from endowments by her zealous members in
past ages, and is no more the property of the nation, than the
land of any private individual or corporation. If this immemorial
endowment of the Church of England be taken away by an act of
the State, what security have we left for any other ancient endowment, or indeed any property whatever?
When the Dissenters' Chapels Bill, by which it was proposed
to alienate the endowments of many chapels, was before Parliament seventeen years ago, the " *Committee of Protestant Dissenting Congregations in or near London*" sent up a petition, in
which they affirm that " they have observed with anxiety and
alarm the introduction of the Bill by which they conceive the
rights of property are dangerously violated." In the petition from
the " *Congregational Union of England and Wales*," at that time
representing one thousand eight hundred congregations, " The
petitioners enter their decided protest against the passing of the
measure, *deeming it a flagrant violation of long-established and
acknowledged rights*, and forming a most dangerous precedent for
future interferences by the legislature with religious trust; the
adoption of such a rule *would give a legal sanction to the most
profane uses of places of public worship.*" Other equally strong
passages from these petitions may be found in Mr. Clifford's lecture
referred to at page 12. Is it then wrong to rob the dissenters and
right to rob the Church? Or have the dissenters changed their
principles in the last seventeen years? Are they ready now to
give up their endowments?

Note I.—*William Cobbett on the Established Church.*

The following shrewd remarks of William Cobbett do not give
the highest view of an Established Church; but they are well
worthy of consideration:—

" *Ought we to have any Establishment at all ?* In answering which for ourselves, it is our own opinion that this nation has been much more religious and happy under the influence of the Protestant Established Church, than it is ever likely to be in case that Church were abolished. To make the question still more close, let it be this: *whether it be reasonable that any one should be called upon to contribute towards the maintenance of a Church, the tenets of which he dissents from ?* This is making the question as home as it can well be. And we do not hesitate to say, that there is to us nothing so outrageously unreasonable in the idea. One thing is certain, that if *all* are not to remain liable to pay for the Church, it is no Established, or at least no *National* Church. Reasons are not wanting to shew the benefits of a national religion, or a mode of worship, or some religious establishment, the peculiarites of which are under the especial patronage and peculiar favour of the government. In judging of such a matter, we can only be guided by experience; and experience is not less wisdom here than in all other things.''

" It does not follow that because an Institution has been abused it should be done away with, if the Institution itself be necessary or beneficial. Even kings may require now and then to be driven from their thrones ; but that does not prove the necessity of doing away with the throne.''

" If it be allowed (and we think it ought to be) that an Establishment is desirable for such a purpose, the dissenters cannot well object to paying the clergy of a different persuasion. An Establishment cannot consist of *all creeds*, or the Quakers themselves would have a right to form a part of it. As we have before said, the Church is not *national* unless *all* be taxed towards its support ; and for the sake alone of preserving decency for religion, it appears to us to be no more unjust than it is impolitic towards the community in general, to require the aid of *all* in maintaining that in which *all* are equally interested.''

" But then come the just and charitable principles of the Christian religion ; and they say this to the owners of the land and the houses; the land and the houses are yours, but not in such absolute right as to exclude your working and poorer brethren from all share. There shall be a Church in each parish, and a priest for the teaching of religion ; there shall be a churchyard for the burial of the dead ; there shall be sermons, and prayers, and marriages, and baptisms, and these shall form the possessions of the inhabitants, the property of those who labour.''

" Go upon a hill, *if you can find one*, in Suffolk or Norfolk ; and you can find plenty in Hampshire, or Devonshire and Wiltshire ; look to the Church steeples, one in almost every four square miles at the most on an average—imagine a man of small learning at the least, to be living in a genteel and commodious house, by the side of every one of these steeples, almost always with a wife and family ; always with servants, natives of the parish, gardener, groom, at the least, and all other servants. A large farm-yard, barns, stables, thrashers, a carter or two, more or less of glebe and of farming.

Imagine this gentleman having an interest, an immediate and pressing interest in the productiveness of every field in his parish—being probably the largest corn-seller in the parish, and the largest rate-payer —more deeply interested than any other man can possibly be in the happiness, harmony, morals, industry, and sobriety of the people in his parish. Imagine his innumerable occasions of doing acts of kindness; his immense power in preventing the strong from oppressing the weak, his salutary influence coming between the hard farmer, if there be one in his parish, and the feeble or simple-minded labourer. Imagine all this to exist close alongside of every one of these steeples, and you will at once say to yourself, hurricanes and earthquakes must destroy the island before that Church can be overthrown. And when you add to all this, that this gentleman, besides the example of good manners, of mildness and of justice, that his life and conversation are constantly keeping before the eye of his parishioners—when you add to all this, that one day in every week he has them assembled together to sit in silence, to receive his advice, his admonitions, his interpretation of the will of God as applicable to their conduct and their affairs; and that too in an edifice rendered sacred in their eyes, from their knowing that their forefathers assembled there in ages past, and from its being surrounded by the graves of their kindred—when this is added, and when it is recollected that the children pass through his hands at their baptism, that it is he alone who celebrates the marriages, and performs the last sad service over the graves of the dead; when you think of all this, it is too much to believe that such a Church can fall. Yet fall it will," &c.

" This settles the matter as to the Church as it now stands; and then the next question is, ' *Can it be restored to what it ought to be ;* ' If it could be, that is the thing that ought to be done—because, though people in great towns do not perceive it, it is a serious change to the country, a serious change to the 465 parishes of Devonshire for instance, to the 629 parishes of Lincoln, the 731 parishes of Norfolk, the 411 parishes of Kent—a serious change to take away one little gentleman out of every one of these parishes."—Cobbett's "*Political Register*," as quoted in the notes to Chalmers' Lectures.

Since the days of Cobbett, the Church has laid much firmer hold of the affections of the people. We have not the slightest fear that as a Church, or as an Establishment, it will fall. The favouring Providence of God will, we believe, continue to defend this country from what, as the above passage shews, Cobbett would have held to be the great national calamity of the separation of Church and State.

THE END.

THOMAS MELLARD, PRINTER, STOURBRIDGE.

www.ingramcontent.com/pod-product-compliance
Lightning Source LLC
Chambersburg PA
CBHW030720110426
42739CB00030B/1040